MATRIC RAGE

POEMS BY

GENNA GARDINI

UHLANGA NEW POETS

2015

Matric Rage
Part of the uHlanga New Poets series
© Genna Gardini 2015, all rights reserved

Published in Cape Town, South Africa by uHlanga in 2015
uhlangapress.co.za

Distributed outside South Africa by African Books Collective
africanbookscollective.com

ISBN: 978-0-620-67692-2

Cover image by Nick Mulgrew
Cover illustration by Alice Edy

The body text of this book is set at 10pt/15pt in Didot HTF 11

ACKNOWLEDGEMENTS

The first versions of some of the poems in this book originally appeared
in the following magazines, websites and anthologies: *New Coin, New
Contrast, Carapace, Prufrock, ITCH, Aerodrome, uHlanga, African
Writing Online, Sometimes, Sentinel Literary Quarterly, The Common,*
the *Sober and Lonely Library for Science Fiction & Feminism & Misc.,*
and Feminists SA. I would like to thank the editors of these publications.

Special thanks to my publisher and editor Nick Mulgrew, for his
abiding belief in my poetry, his own poetry, and his patience.

I would also like to thank the following: Colleen Higgs for selecting
"The Pot" for the 2012 DALRO *New Coin* Prize, the Sol Plaatje/
European Union Poetry Award for publishing some of my poems in
their anthologies in 2011, 2012, 2013 and 2015, and PEN SA for choosing
"Performance Scale" as one of their two official entries to the 2015 PEN
International/New Voices Award.

I owe so much to so many, starting with Erica Lombard and Christie
Towers for being the first real readers and critics of my work as a
makeshift teenage online poetry collective.

My other friends, who have read, performed and lived so many
drafts of these poems (and also allowed me to use them as a constant
excuse not to go out) – Gary Hartley, Emma de Wet, Siya Ngcobo, Byron
James Davis, Ella Scheepers, Xoli Matomela, Rosemary Lombard, Amy
Louise Wilson, Elizabeth Munro, Qanita Smith, Michelle du Plessis, Mdu
Kweyama, Rosa Rogers Postlethwaite, Kate Abney, Arthur Mataruse,
Kate Arthur, Bianca Camminga, Zanne Solomon, Roger Young, and
Robert Haxton.

My teachers, past and present – Sara Matchett, Janet Buckland,
Reza de Wet, Aryan Kaganof, Justine Loots, Winsome Pinnock, Elyse
Dodgson, and Malika Ndlovu.

My 2015 first-year degree writing students, who remind me why poetry is necessary. My medical team, Dr. Colin Wolpe, Dr. Dion Opperman, Sally Shannon, and Sandra Joubert, who perhaps do the same thing, although in a different way.

My beloved Nonno, Gino Dalla Pria, whose stories have stayed with me since my childhood. My dear cousins, Carla and Gabriella Fedetto.

My partner and great love, Roxy Kawitzky.

Finally, and most of all, my parents, Mara and Oscar Gardini, who gave me everything.

— G.G.

The publication of this book was made possible due partly to a grant by Nedbank Arts Affinity through the Arts & Culture Trust. uHlanga would like to express their gratitude to both institutions.

CONTENTS

For my family: Mara Gardini, Oscar Gardini and Roxy Kawitzky

The Pot

This is what's sewn into the colon's brick lining:
I, my own darling, am monstrous marvelous made.

I count out my turns from the curd in dog years.
I am many stamps due and fixed like a bud to the spine,
fit to bloom.

I, snail-sum, will burn! I, signal, am post!
I'd fill myself fifty before I quash at that trough
which is the pit and the nucleus. Which is the back of your skirt.

I, little meat cleat, have stacked up my genes like spare business cards.
I wrought clean out of knowing and moved moth-muscles to say:

Of all the strange things time has gurgled from its silt,
I will string **this** to my collar. I will lock it to my nape.

Horror's not the seedling. It's the pot. It's the pot!
There are things that I planted. There are things I will not.

JUNIOR

The Archivist

The past clicks us into focus.
There's a slid-hinge to the edit.

In this photo, your father frames you
like a fish he wants to remember –
slipped and tin, temporarily pliable,
propped on his knee.

Let's take your brother, here,
blue-faced and stuffed, full of berries out the
bottom of the backyard, off the bramble
of his foot, rolling from the cabinet's
carpet like a gum to its tongue,
small and sand-favoured;

his cheek still a linen chest of flesh
before he turned himself down

for girls who developed with their legs poised
stern as oars. They were his wife. Their skirts
unassailable septums, bone-walled. And their
factory-lit health, a tithe

I find myself paying,

and saying, "Well, what's honest is what lines it:
the advertorial milk blanket of your insides."

While my friends ask, "Is this how shit always is?"
and listen, and wonder what fresh therapist
will chug the construction belt of their counsel,
tap court shoes square and cocked, to knock
the morse code of medication, and send us
nearing ourselves, for three months, or about.

So I smoke the scalpel of memory instead,
and scour love in its clot, as time consults
like a ruler. And each inch knows this
is the telling. This is the business of my life:

to talk that bread out of its dripping
with the small, sauced animal of my knife.

The Evil Eye

You cannot compare a place called Benoni
to one named Waterfall.

This is what I learnt when I was six,
as we left the flat, beige tablecloth
of the Rynfield hinterland –
where what the real estate agent grinned was grass
proved instead a Mica mat of woodchips,
biting at my Toughees
the way our maltese poodle Scampie often did –
for a town my waving Zias sighed was "the sticks."

But our new house by the gorge,
gaping like a fresh cavity in a jaw,
wasn't snapping or thin,
but green and wet like a Creme Soda float,
or dug and bursting as a zit.
Mom, clutching the cross she intended to affix
in the breakfast nook,
kept repeating that we now had a full one-acre plot.
I did not know what that meant, but I knew it must be a lot.

After a year, defeated by the heat,
Scampie half-darted between monkeys and trees
like it was Athletics Day but he was only going for bronze.
Dad's work shirts would come home drenched as a dishcloth,
lapping at the day like air rushing to the brain,
like Carlton paper embracing a stain.

"It's just the moisture in this bloody place!" Mom would say,
"Everything is crying here, don't think it's just you, feel the walls!"

Alone, I ran my fingers, already soiled
by the plants I urged seeds from,
whispering "Look, it also poos!"
along the side of the laundry room.
I wasn't meant to go near that squat structure
because the neighbours hissed there was an evil eye
painted at the back. I inched out through a gap
that would later lead Scampie free then under a bakkie,
squinting my own fixed gaze to see
the promised sinful iris glaring properly.
Women in Day-Glo takkies jogged past, whistling
"Hi koeks, but where's your nanny?"

The corner of the wall bore no cornea.
Instead it was plain and shut as a lid.
But when I placed my scrunched fist,
each time a little bigger, against it,
I could feel something there,
see-through but steady, sure
as it dripped.

Horses' Heads

Try sit me by the Afrikaans boy,
match our stretchmarks with tongues,

and watch: we will only learn to love each other,
rud-fisted, phonetically.

My mother didn't understand the teacher,
who kept a china plate in place of her palate;

but then she couldn't follow all the implied italics
in the harp-dipped mountains, either.

So we didn't move back to the old country
(which it really was,

the plane full of your Zias,
gold-rimmed and permanent, even in economy,

looking the way they always did to you:
like money on a farm)

or stay in the ticker-tape dentist's office
that was her Harare,

settling out and up, instead,
monkeys, and your brother, wild in our acre.

Please don't chastise me
for having read my olive skin off

like you think if I aired all my sun'd linen
I'd be any less of a white.

First Generation

Where I am from we do not measure relation in corpuscles.

That is why I love you more than I know how to tell you
and I tell you all the time

about the tiny Canadian
demonstrating the sting of the felt mantis.
He mouths it into your puppet's pursed ear.
Oh, Jesus,
your mother and your father and your brother,
your Nonna who soiled her gingham dress
in glee by the ProNutro pool at the old house,
in Zimbabwe. One day, I, also, will realise
I am a grown woman
being chased by a monkey, and wee.

Bone memories speak a language of marrow, fried.
We were made for the government school,
the horse-prowled Benoni farmlands,
an uncle's 7-Eleven down by the train tracks.

She told me that I grew in her heart
instead of under it,
and I imagined myself squashed in that cavity,
sucking on a cardiac chord, like a slikkie.
More than blood, more than fat.
I am made of these moments,

healthy as cells, with their new-mattress walls bolstered
by decades of cutlery and jars, the Lazy Susan
we spun to Durban and Cape Town and back –
a roulette I won, every time.

Il Diavolo

On our way to King Shaka Airport,
past the road's touristing ribcage of tusks,
through the toll rising priced and plonked on the corner
like hard plastic pushed in play-dough, my Mom tells me about
her first time seeing the happy-clappies.

When her Daddy remarried, her new step-mother (or Zia,
as she still calls her) shook the Pope from him like a rock
out a slop. They began to attend, instead, one of those
Evangelicals, a place hemmed with the hum of immigrants,
cheeseclothed people pulsing, privately, in a tent.

On this night, they took my Mom, who'd lost her own
one year before. The space where her family had been,
sleeved as if an arm, and pushing. She was fifteen

when she watched those congregants clutch and convulse
like the Camry my Pop would later teach her to drive: viscous
under their tops, something in them rubberising bone, leaking
and reaching towards her as they moaned, "Il Diavolo! Il Diavolo!"

She raised us Catholic.

For Laura (who is four)

We have drawn a picture of you, together.

My little, my white plaster cast, unfloured,
a first-year installation, a story I read before doo-doo,
watching you glass eye watch me,
the chink-wall of channels, shuffling.

You will not sleep,
have to tell me about each item in your toy box.
"I love it!" That tiny chest, straining towards things,
I love it.

This is my one hair (*What happened to the rest?*
They burned it in the fires, you shrug,
but before I can ask) and this is my dress (*I know,
I helped with that part.* Yes, you did, grudgingly)
and this my winky.

Ah, fat oblong. I took you for a slipper.

You still expect me in the cubicle,
that small hot hand, limp and protesting in mine,
the resigned murmur of "Uppies" when there are too
many spikes in this hanging basket of a yard,
being big, being useful.

You sure you have a winky?
Ja, I do.

I see a circle on the sternum, un-toured.
S'that, baba? It's where I got bitened.

Hey?

We only change the sheets for when you dream
of your small mouse trapped in the parrot's cage
and wake up, missing! This talcum powder give,
this springy.

You try again –

You know, you know when the wolf bitened me?
You know when the wolf and the ghost bitened me? –
You peel a bandage from my finger,
sit it on the sketch's collarbone.

Owie? I hazard.
Owie, you confirm.

Bedtime Stories

Time's licked me like a nut, and right to the inside.

Once, strange hands furred us down
and we were the nodes on furious mice.

Now, I operate from this, the dust-kitchen of my lap,
like a cook on conference call,

stellactating. I am bed-iced and sore.
A splinter, but sopping.

Little girl, climbed right between the nubs,
fretted my belly till it caved, loved me knowing

and unknowing I had grown our blood
sequestered. In rows, like mushrooms.

When you were a child we played clean as kettles
and I prized the print-press of your limbs, and skin,

because my looking read your living out:
face fleshy, little pig's toe, fanny furled into a truffle.

But now, you've woken up, foot-wrinkled, and steaming

with the old game, caught arm down, wearing bite rungs
like chromosomes, saying

there are more ways to sully a sheet than with sleeping,
hey! as if I had chopped you out of nothing.

You ask the wrong question when you
ask about the wolf.

Mister

Mister, you crinkle off my brocks
like a yellow sucker wrapper,
calling me precious
(or precocious, I can't tell which
with the crackle of this cellophane hymen
caught snapping like a lid on your mouth.)

You are as thready as a wear in the leather,
puffing from the crook of your collapsed chin,
asking to let you run one of my powder stockings,
cobbled, down your shin

until, with one fowled swoop of your sciatic,
Methuselastic,
hip-replacement-in-the-attic arm,
you sit me slap on your knee. "How old are we?" say "Pretty,
pretty in your yellow dress!"
(And, of course, you can guess the rest.)

I am bucked and perched, my bit chest fresh,
my patent white feet swinging wide-soled and sweet,
while one finger, thick and sticky as a popsicle,
is slid in to check if the dough is ready.

But you like to crack the inside soft,
with a little time to spare,
and I find your tweed hands itching and
plying my two dumpling knees apart
as if to trace by heart a start on a sore
that isn't even a scab, yet.

I could slip you in, flaccid, to the side, I offer,
but it seems there's cutting in you still
(or, at least, enough to slick one smooth slice between.)
So I seep you all out, mister, yellow and mean.

SENIOR

Sharks Board

Even in 1996,
this blonde marine biologist
says the words "Great White"
like he is introducing himself.

I am in Grade 4.
My class has been shuttled off
to the Sharks Board,
clutching indemnity forms
that fumble the term
"excursion"

as if they know an "outing",
which to our parents could only mean
metal through the wrong lobe
glinting off a strobe light;
is, for a child, a foefie-slide ride
past the exit sign

and out the fire escape.
We scaled towards and down
those days like ants
from a fog of fumigation.

The marine biologist, flexing,
feels at and flops loose a shark,
dead,
for us to see,
its body making noises against the slab
like wet vegetables on a counter.

I think of the fish's mouth
as that of a woman in a portrait,
resigned. The man pries at it
with one unkind, prophylactic digit,
demonstrating that it can't contract
or choose, the way that art does,
but must be revealed forcibly,
against context.

He jimmies out a tooth,
holds it up
like a jeweler would a diamond.
We are dismayed

at the black hole he's arranged
in the glove of the shark's head,
where once, like a hangnail,
intention had snatched and bit.
We press our own small fingers
into it

while the biologist lifts his scalpel
to the tire texture of its side
and slits. Like that *Star Wars* scene,
the innards worm and steam
around us. "Now look what she eats!"
he recites as if from a script,
and this, I can tell, is the point
of the trip:

that the contents are all plastic.

What plops, knotted and stuck
from the stomach seems
a Tupperware tumor.
A toy mushroom wrapped in snot.

Its head averted, the shark
is the only one not shocked
as the biologist sweeps its flesh
along a bin, then indicates we should leave
the same way we came in.

Outside,
a snapping cement version
twists and dives
above us.

How I Hate You

How I hate you, other girl,
is not how I hate myself.

It's not even how I hate the story
you want to hear while we bunk PE,

imagining me soaking at your shoulder
like it is a desert and my apology is the hose.

I am not some rubber attached to a tap.
I am not even the tap.

I am the whole fucking hydration system.

I am the reservoir dug low in your thinking
and piped back through your brain.

I am the structure that keeps you flicking
and alive,

that gives you the sense to even know you
are in pain.

I am the dam. You build me because you want me.

You see your own face, which is never my face,
across the surface of it and understand

that how I hate you
is how I look at you at all.

Angry Girl

You say my anger squats and rises in me
like a stale loaf, half-baked
on the low rung of a broken oven,
its steel trays slamming and wincing
through the hinges,
like so many mouths in braces

(not saying: fists against faces.)

Or that my anger flops on the world
like an off pie,
collapsing in the middle,
the kind you'd decapitate at break-time
to attack only from the inside.
"Besides, eating this is basically like
having ten slices of bread," you'd smirk,
monitoring each mouthful

(not saying: through a jaw forced open.)

But, actually:

My anger doesn't irritate or itch.
Because it's a fact, you see, not a glitch.
Comforting, it folds and separates,
like sheets, like a duvet,
and in it I stuff each dismissal away.
I press the push buttons to seal it,

small and reshaped.
I tuck it in at the edges.
I remake it every morning.

My anger flares down time,
fast as a fish
caught in another sort of current,
electric and silvered,
not with scale but reflection.
You consider it catched,
snatched and still in your net.
Not admitting it's vibrating,
never saying it's not dead.

My anger moves as if ash
down your institutional passage,
staining each surface,
fingering the walls.
It doesn't ask permission to travel
because fire never does.
All my anger requires
is some sort of friction,
a tension solved by air.
A gasp, I guess,
at the kindling you levered
from legs pushed apart
into small stacks you'd hacked,
sure the pyre was the point,
sure containment was ahead.

Forgetting that flames spread.

Whale Watching

The concept of size can never exist for a whale
because the sea will always scale to accommodate it,

like a parent at the crib, smoothing and settling
a comforter or bib; a preventative cloth caught
light on the skin, only daring to move
if the creature within might.

Under the ocean, even a whale is small enough
for the luxury of privacy, able to hide and dive
inside litres of time.

This is why when you say, "Don't you think – *hey!*
Don't you think so-and-so looks like a beached whale?"
what you're actually blurting about isn't blubber
burnt to bone, but a lament against context:

recognizing that something larger than you,
and outside of your language, rose in tandem
without tongue, an absence used as if a blade
in a suicidal pact against place.

"What are you doing here?" our matron asked
the girls a grade below, who then glassed and glared
toward me. "Whale watching," they reply.

Goodbye to Rosie

For Rosemary Lombard

This girl and this man sing together.

They are sitting on these steps,
which for them, which for me,
must also in some way be a stage,
a scrim set defined by a door shut behind
the camera's squint squiz;
the gap between her space and his
grouted and flat,
locked like a spine snapped
between wings.

Complicating the exit.

It is early in the morning.
He has been asked to come and play music for,
no, with children. On television. On these stairs
which lead to the sort of porch (I write "stoop")
that he has lately been avoiding.
But today he hovers near it, near her,
and says, and stops himself from saying,
that it was a brownstone (in my tongue,
a "townhouse") like this where he'd first met his wife,

who tipped into him as stiff and iceless
as the drink he couldn't buy her then.
He thought she would open up
as if an elevator in the building of conversation,
a device he could ride from across to sides
without ever having to construct a scaffold himself.
(I'd say "lift.") He was wrong.
She divorced him a year before.
Now his problems are like his hair, parted.

He is 38. The girl is seven, or six.
They've asked her to come and sit,
to come and sing with him.
She says hello, ducks her head,
small animal, small pump of blood
and possibility. She is made
of corduroy, he thinks, soft,
un-malleably furrowed. Without zip.
He can appreciate her wholeness,
he is weary of it.

He himself feels fetched,
feels stitched from thin material,
worrying at the connections.
You can see the marks of the alterations
he made, or let others make, on his ancient guitar,
whose strings knot and flay where he has pulled at them.
This does not seem beautiful to him.
He won't ever get another.

The song is about an event he refuses to explain
to the girl,
so he tries to only pronounce words like
"mamma" or "pyjama" –
leaving them placed sweet,
as if icing on a cake,
praying "Let her life lick past it" –
when, suddenly, she yells,
"Dance! Dance! Dance!"

The man is concerned, he interrupts her,
but she tries again, when the lenses turn,
this time pointing at him while humming:
"Look! I can see the bird!"

Two decades later, a friend will post
a link to this on my Facebook wall.
And I'll think, "She wasn't wrong at all!"
And I'll think, "I'm nothing like you."

On Words

She said, "Love, the only thing that lives is letters."

The truth is a clamour, is a great rocking vibration
that's brittle and sex-shelled; that's listening, a conch.

I've looked into that mouth, and asked: Did I know you
from my self's start?

From the first crustacean dollop of my brain, where both
the speaking and the tongue are still sitting, undrained?

Our lives wonder each other, disassemble like engines,
the process sudden, apparent.

Stop mid-speech, take the motor out your talk.

Click the conversation from its context into a grammar
that even your mother used like false teeth: a means to an end
she could take off at night. Only knowing herself when she
was just gums.

Words shamed me, so I loved them.

Laundered and spelt, I've felt each sentence as strain,
a thin membrane pulled between throat and head until
I called from the nodes of my chest, instead, humming:
Is this where I learn into myself?

Already the writing sheets above me, cursive and prophesying,
doing meaning mean justice, double-stitched against time.

But sometimes here,

but sometimes here you'll talk of language like a lover,
like a white-wash of water outside a church in the Karoo.

And this is how it separates you.

HIGH

Blackberry

Siya handles his Blackberry like it's a small child,
mother-board and horizontal. He names it Bill,
clicks it into its crib, letting the noise of that fit
seal and connect the air, like a monitor.

When Bill breaks, he carries it into my room,
the cover of his hands cupped, a cot.

I put my finger to its face, which is foreign
and blinking, which is remindful of options
outside the manual. "Fucked," Siya tells me.

Out

This girl sits down opposite me,

her shirt white and riding the space between the passage door
and the bed. Slipping out the packaging like something just soaped
and now asleep in its towel. Expanding, as I count the thread.

She swivels, closer, in her chair.

And there's this canine flash of content. What hides beneath
the hamper and its lid. Her skin is packed like a fresh steak
of rubber. Like a piece of untreated whalebone. Like a fin.
Turning me left as I wouldn't aim in to wanting to touch
the place where her clothes had lifted.

I remember saying this must be an easier thing for other people.

When I think of us as younger, as fourteen,
I think of your small but forever body causing something in me
to stir, which I called (and wrote) maternal so I had an excuse
to touch it, monitoring my hands but never my mouth, loving you
and terrified of you because your judgement was like your face,
both pocked and cyclical.

It's this I came to and went from. Wrecking,

ashamed of what'd happened in the spare room at your Auntie Pam's,
where I had to do the dipping because you wouldn't play the man,
envying you your blonde and wanness, your shock at reading the *YOU*
magazine phrase for what we did against your Ouma's historical
    lampshade,

wanting your reluctance, also, for myself.

Secular Girl

My body splits like a fish.
I slipped these facts from my flesh
and jerked their glands out for sex
in the cinema of synapse.

Loss kept you locked, like a tampon.
But, look, so can my tongue.
I'll pitch you loose from that collar,
you'll strip the clotting off my gums.

We'll wave the wounds we worked for arms,
press our parts against our parts,
have the same constant conversation
between this crotch and that heart,

instead of talking what flight or movement
could make. I part my dandruff and say we
were the chaff of God's thigh! When all I hurtle
now's a trunk;

is this false and testing body.

The Common-Law Wife

Back then,

when time was still a needle at our thigh
and we clamped for each other like corsets,

we were conjugal.

Now, I, column and alarm, light your smokes
but not your arms.

I've stiffed my spine against this maw until its
moving bound me, mandible.

Kept me bolted to the bone.

Love, the pink, un-certificate stamp of my pain,
is a thing that you cooked. First to eat,

then flush away.

Indemnity Form

On the morning of the day you'd leave

– for what neither of us knew, then, would be a stretch
marked thick and clear as a screen; a cord gnawed to fibres
by space intervened;

of only being linked by a dominoing deck of avatars,
collapse implied in the gaps between views – I woke up late
for work, tried to jerk my arm out from under the duvet and
found that what I was under was you.

Probably the third or fourth time we fucked,

I remember looking up and finding you, still drunk,
your expression catching and used as a baseball mitt
(something imported, waiting for the inevitable to hit),
miming what I was doing to you.

You shadowed it above my head, fractioning space with movement,
dividing the firmament like a bank teller. (What gesture is before it dumbs
to skin. What measure makes in margins.) And I thought it seemed
as if you were trying to sign out of us. Autographing the air

like an indemnity form.

Art Critic at the Beach

This seaweed is just spool.

It's green and long as a projector's tongue. And the rock it's on
seems plastic-knifed. Disemboweled, like an old VHS. It doesn't work
for me.

But then, suddenly, the sea arrives and edits the scene out, awkwardly
washing towards, replacing. I have my suspicions about the whole
thing

and scan the horizon for junior curators. And parking.

Down-a-ways, my girlfriend plays at the tide while I find some paper
to put this on. She kneels and welcomes the water:

I think she's sure I'm writing about her now, her body angled
so I may describe the ocean as it fleshes fresh her every part.
Is she checking if I missed that? It's no problem, she can restart.

She raises her hand to a wave, the reception of her face stopped,
her arm stick and familiar. (She beaming "Ariel!" I scribbling "mop.")
I'm fairly certain she's not noticed the condom tangling near her slop.

I'll wait for her to walk back.

The Aquasize Instructor

She just doesn't like the look of me,
I can tell,

with my face dripping from this cap, as if twisted from a tap
into a shallow pool of fat

that gathers twice at the chin.
It's the gusset of ancient stockings you handmade.

I'm screwed out of my body, like a bulb.

On the first day, she berates me for not breathing properly –
says, "If you want to look like *this*, you must be healthy!" –

her body jerking in its costume, like biltong in a condom.

I duck down into the deep-end and, snorkeling, mouth,
"I'm not this moment. I'm its document. I'll last longer!"

while old men thunder and tool towards me: sea bulls,
snapped back to movement by the water,

which does not hum and wait the way the world does,
inferring

and ushering you to death in a series of past bedrooms,
old lovers dropping from the windows like stompies.

Above, the instructor steams and strives. Furious
as a fish in a microwave, she tells the ladies "I'm 45!"

and waits for their reactions. They pause,

then titter. They are polite. Tonight, they'll talk
to their husbands of her calves, risen and fingered

like rolls they wouldn't buy at the Woolworths.

She catches me smirking and I want to say:
"See, I'm no longer cleft like a sum by this abacus of bone.

I'm inking time in metres! My brain sinks two! It clicks,
then switches.

Hungry as scissors for fingers!" But she looks away.

On Guilt

You say guilt has solved a rod out of your spine.
Well, it only ever made a fucking fossil of mine!

Jammed its spit up my current, rift my petting for a chord.

It cups me, fatty as old cotton. It plots an outline of my pipes,

while I fasten my membranes, quick as a purse.
When I fisted my lap at myself, like a pocket, and
rattled your faces in it, for change, I wanted to say:

"I'll sting out a cave clean from this breath!
I'll pop every prospect like it was a testicle!"

My pride retains because I calcify it.

Chalked with speech, I dorsal markers at each knee.
So slit, loss fits; knows the heft of tits packed with hessian.
The septic flowers time can stain on skin.

I've passed you over gum and root. I've pushed you,
puckered, through my gut.

I take what I need from you.

Bleed Us Not Into Temptation

Behind the concertina door of this room divider,
which folds and gathers, impractical as a paper fan,
I contemplate the Rorschach test pressed against
my sanitary pad.

Peeling away from my panties
as if a traffic officer from a car crash,
its flaps snap back at me,
incisors guarding a great gullet.

The plasma is patted past this material,
like a small swell intercepted by a reef;
like a bruised face beyond a veil, pixelated
in its grief.

And I understand, for the first time maybe,
why in adverts a woman's hand
is edited from her body,
and forced to enter a frame

that is split in half like a window (and perhaps
this is why they call them period panes?)
to divest a beaker of its thin blue liquid
into a stack of un-thighed thickness.

This frothless formula is a man-made wave,
cleft without smell, out of inherited shame,
secreted under a smooth skirt sketched by suggestion.
No legs meshed to chafe, no visible irritation, no blood

to spoil an image which draws at conclusion
without the rubber of representation.
These smiling TV girls sing for someone else's gain.
Like a placebo boiled out a Bunsen burner,
they are decorative,

and through them I see the VAT-heavy shape
of the box, with edges tucked, not ripped.
The prospect of its clean and cotton contents
move to mute all lips.

I change the channel.
Later, I pick small clots of myself,
as if crops out the seeping plain of my lap.
Like a sponge, I regenerate, right away.

Fat

You cannot be liked

You cannot be loved

You cannot have sex

You cannot have *good* sex

You cannot fuck the people you want – well,

You cannot *really* have wanted to fuck them, then

You cannot live a long life. I mean, that's a medical fact, so don't even start

You cannot pose nude for art

You cannot like clothes

You cannot be in these photos

You cannot get married. Sorry? OK, so

You cannot want to get married because you're trying to convince me
    it's your choice instead of his – hey?

You cannot be gay. You're only saying that because you're sure no man
    would ever choose

You cannot have children because it's genetic

You cannot blame genetics because you're just lazy

You cannot have issues, that's such an easy excuse

You cannot enjoy food! I enjoy food, your friends enjoy food, Nigella
    enjoys food – and we don't look like

You cannot get yelled at in the street. Alright, you *can* get yelled at in
    the street but it will always be about this and not

You cannot ask me to stop because I'm just joking and lighten up and
    see what I did there

You cannot tell me it's not my place to say so when it's your health I'm
    thinking of

You cannot think properly because there are too many layers blocking
     your brain
You cannot be so cushioned and say you are in pain
You cannot do anything but write because you only have to use your
     fingers for that. Look at your cousin, she abseils
You cannot be good at maths or you would know what you add up to on
     the scale of
You cannot get to heaven because how would you climb all those stairs
You cannot believe in God because the rest of you is in the way. If there
     was less you'd believe in more
You cannot shop in this store
You cannot be told that you look beautiful without me muttering "for..."
You cannot go to Paris (it's in their visa requirements)
You cannot survive in the Antarctic
You cannot survive in the Atlantic
You cannot survive me
You cannot achieve anything without them saying "Good for her, but
     what a pity she"
You cannot touch yourself (how would you reach?)
You cannot let someone else touch you
You cannot let someone else not touch you
You cannot be telling the truth, why would he do that to *you* when he
     could have any other
You cannot fit into this skin I made for
You cannot wear that swimsuit because
You cannot cut your hair so short, what will distract them from
You cannot have a problem that is not caused by
You cannot understand that you'd be so much happier if you'd just lose
You cannot still be so unhappy, after all that, maybe you just need to

You cannot talk about the things you thought you couldn't have and
    couldn't do like it was such a big deal you managed to work your
    way through (you are the big deal, literally), like it took you till
    now, from when you were only a kid to realise *I* was the weight you
    needed to be rid of. Honestly,
You cannot be so sensitive when we all know that this isn't what I mean
    every time I call you

fat.

MATRIC

Matric Rage

On the day we wrote our last exam,
we took off to the sea

in a convoy of our fathers' old Mercedes,
perched along the seats' laps like safety pins
half stuck in. Singular but fastening.
We called it our Matric Rage,
which I thought sounded accurate.

Once arrived, my friends went to visit,
then were visited by, this fast blink of boys
who named us "The Nuns" because we froze
then thawed out dinners nightly
in the holiday-house dance of our mums.
Knowing the comforts of a placemat
in the face of what comes.
After they left, we played 30 Seconds all night,
slept Tetrised in too few beds. Tucked together
chastely, chastely.

On our last evening we arrived at theirs
and found another girl on the balcony, passed out
into the front of her gentleman IEB candidate.
She was younger (I remember thinking, fifteen?
That tipping age) but with him in a way none of us
had ever been. Even you, our most dented,
kept your virginity on like a Ricoffy lid,
bubbling at the hand but sealed where it counts.

Here, all of a sudden, was the real arm-haired business of sex.
Sitting separate from us. Staying the night.

He nudged her awake, helped her up,
the sloping straps of her top
as significant and illegible to me
as the road signs I'd seen the day before
on that same beach

when I moved along it with you

and knew how even rocks could dilate
like an eye behind a frame.
Now dull and lidded,
now open in the shade
of the spaces you were certain
only circumstance had made
(which were permanent
to me).

There is always some small give to be used.

And each temporary crock,
each accommodating trough,
was small and private enough;
a place where things could be performed;
where evidence could be wrung;
where you could leave the water quick
with what we'd just done to it,
and walk back to the others,

dry, in your towel, in your bikini.

Dressage

The day I knew I could love you,
you sat side and over me like I was
your pony, an animal to buck ridden
under. Not broken in the way shoes are
forced to forget their first form, convinced
they've always been bone and flesh by the constant
press of weight, but clicked the way a latch has to stay
hinged from the bar to make a gate. You drove me
through. Time was our vehicle, packed to carry us
alone. Then bare-backed but pastured, when stable
now home.

The day I knew you could love me,
I took down the dress which had clung
from my door like paint should, for years,
fixed by memory: the shopkeeper holding to halve
her fears and my fist which she found too thematically thick
with rands to risk. Who could measure such a waist? She hissed,
"Sweetie, be serious. You can't really think it will fit?"
But I did and I do, because it fit you.
You pulled it on like you would me, carefully.
Your hands finding and pushing past each space,
understanding that needles use gaps to make lace,
the material close and separate. Near as your skin,
as far.

The Narcissist's Guide to Electronics

I've always secretly believed
that my body is a TV
and time its old decoder,

filtering through history
to blink, fuzzy and momentary,
on my monitor

until, overcome by static,
both machines go blank.

Remember,
no channel can be viewed
without a screen.

Performance Scale

1:

I spent so many years attacking my body,
finding fault in faint abundance, obsessing over every lack
that it didn't surprise me when I woke up one morning
to discover that it was finally fighting me back.

2:

This was the year you kept killing all the machines you owned
and that is what we refer to as a "running motif."
(And *that* is what we refer to as "dramatic irony.")

3:

You'll come to,
conked out on some strange cistern in a Southern Suburbs mall,
your legs hinging against the plastic billboard of the bathroom door,
angled in the jamb like damp cardboard,
folded and forced into a full stop.

4:

This is paper as metaphor and limbs as punctuation.
This is the reverse of writing.

5:

You'll find your phone lying, lesioned, next to you,
a fissure fresh down its crustacean container
like a phantom crack. Like a mime at a wall,
bucking but flat.

6:

You're tipped against a nurse
whose prophylactic palm pats nerved and certain on your neck.
You have heard her tell the others that they are good girls.
You are not a good girl
because when she sets you straight on the mat, then the scale,
she only says, "Try not to hurl," then
"You must make a note of your weight."

7:

The zinging technology of your mouth
steams against the frosted door of the consultation room.

8:

She is warm and alive as an urn at the church fête
and you are the Styrofoam cup
leaning at her tap.

9:

"Look at it this way, at least you'll be skinny!"
is quite a funny thing to say to someone
when you think they could be dying.

10:

You began to let your bob grow unbidden,
split and wrought,
because if a part of your physicality still chooses to thrive
who are you cut it short?

10:

You make these kinds of jokes.

11:

You are convinced that the nails and hair of a corpse
inch out past conclusion, intrepid as weeds, eternal as worms,
eyeless and edging in all directions, past even the last right
to scratch into life. This is poetry, I thought,
before I was told that I was wrong.

12:

You retract back into yourself, creating the illusion of growth,
moving like a skirt hitched above the knee, balking as if in shock,
pressed against the back of the closest ablution block.

13:

At twenty-seven, I became blind in one eye –
but didn't realise, because I only notice my mouth.
I thought perhaps a crack had formed between my head
and the cheese-cloth membrane of my disbelief.

14:

Speaking is uncertain and pinpricked.
It is shrouded. It is grief.

15:

Every bad thing that'd happened to me before
was because a man had decided to teach me a lesson
and this is why, after I found out,
I had to reconsider atheism.

14:

You are turning a manuscript into a
fan with the bridging press of pleats.
You are not Keats.

15:

The good doctor made eye-contact with me for the whole beat,
which I know is supposed to convey the meaningfulness of the
    moment
because of my expensive acting degree.

16:

Raisins injected with water.

17:

Thinned the way paint under the slow drip of turpentine is.

18:

I pick this bed because of its proximity to the TV. I am surrounded by
    women who are in various states of collapse. One spends each day
    lamenting the canteen's slopped and un-broiled chicken à la king,
    sending voice notes to her daughters to remember to let the cat in.
    The others cannot walk. I do not want to know them. I do not want
    to admit that I am one of them. At first, I shuffle, hesitantly, like
    it's a character choice, until I realise I am not performing and the
    gimmick has stuck, gammy. My legs lurch and twitch beyond me.

19:

I look up and there is nothing.

I look down at my own arm, which the nurse has stuck so repeatedly,
    finding me false and veinless, that the blood clotted before it
    gathered, like I was a boring meeting they wanted to leave and this
    might be the exit.

I look up and she is staring straight at me.

Her face is wide and aimed. I pull out my earphones but she is
    whispering. I say her name. She is mouthing something and I do
    not know the words but I know that what she is saying is help me
    and I cannot even help myself

which is why I am plugged into a wall like a faulty Blackberry on
    charge
which is why I am connected to wet metal that looks like a clothes
    horse,
which is why I am making so many Joan Crawford wire hanger jokes.
This means *help me*.

I thumb the call button. The station, which perpendiculates next to
    us, is, unlike myself, without staff. I use the IV as a cane and I call
    out but the movement of my voice is as interrupted as my legs,
    cramped, boned by pain. There is a sound here, it rings out, clean
    and to the side as a scalpel. Panic is a disinfected metal knife, it
    slices me from myself, each thought going into the brain instead
    of the mouth, bounced like an e-mail sent to the incorrect address.
    The prospect of the seizure is thick and electric in her bones, I can
    see it. The day before, her family had come to visit. Two of them
    explained how this latest bout was caused of the evil thoughts she

allowed to enter her head. She must lose them. My own – which buzzed, a constant cortex, old and reliable as a Cortina that has been veering for years, cutting breaks and ties with whoever passed me by – stay stuck. I wish I had a demon but I don't. I have my legs and I run past cornrows of beds to find some assistance

20:

towards the end.

Recycling

My death came for me when I turned twenty-eight.
It said, "Look, I read all your poems,"
then apologised for being late.

One decade before,
I'd pressed and poured my parents' pills
down the utility hose of my throat,
like I was striking a fence or clearing a moat
between my writing and my limbs.
One seemed minded as a mansion
and I wanted to move in,
while the other was base,
a leaking and ledge-less space
where even paper couldn't get past
that fecund first fact of the tree.
Re-rotting and vast, it was a wilderness
with no verse to me
and I schemed, through rhyme,
to escape it.

And sooner – really, maybe ten years prior –
I'd snuck indoors, away
from the chirruping choir of my cousins,
who clawed and contested the bark they were climbing,
broaching branches my own arms refused to bear.
They told me to put down the book, to come get some air.

So, loosed, I learned what happens
when you break the build-up of narrative:
you fall out the bottom of structure.
There I wasn't safe or placed
like insulation below the boards,
but buried, a pip
flattened the way dirt in a vegetable patch is:
just a brief layer beneath all the shit.
Words didn't collapse
into the soft fontanelle of that ditch,
so I thought: no body can avoid this.

Now, the TV chimes, "In today's challenge,
we imagine what we'll eat in 2030!"
and I wonder if I'll still be around to see.
And I understand that it was always
the pallid province of privilege
that afforded me room to feign and swat
like a cockroach against a closed can of Doom,
when really I knew – or thought I knew –
that one slipped step and whole systems of aid
could surely snatch me back,
stroking and sibilant, signing contracts.
But sickness, like the toilet, swallows sweepingly,
with little to no care when I whinge that it's just *so* unfair,
as if this was the only time loss and living would meet;
as if worse things weren't happening mere metres
down the street.

While we wait, it whispers,
"Listen, in the end, what I found
is that even the page and the plant
both land up where they started:
back inside the ground."

also in the UHLANGA NEW POETS SERIES

Failing Maths and My Other Crimes by Thabo Jijana (2015)

————————

also published by UHLANGA

the myth of this is that we're all in this together by Nick Mulgrew (2015)

uhlangapress.co.za

Printed in the United States
By Bookmasters